Recycled Gardens

Written by Katherine Chu

GRL Consultant, Diane Craig,
Certified Literacy Specialist

Lerner Publications ◆ Minneapolis

Note from a GRL Consultant
This Pull Ahead leveled book has been carefully designed for beginning readers. A team of guided reading literacy experts has reviewed and leveled the book to ensure readers pull ahead and experience success.

Copyright © 2025 by Lerner Publishing Group, Inc.

All rights reserved. International copyright secured. No part of this book may be reproduced, stored in a retrieval system, or transmitted in any form or by any means—electronic, mechanical, photocopying, recording, or otherwise—without the prior written permission of Lerner Publishing Group, Inc., except for the inclusion of brief quotations in an acknowledged review.

Lerner Publications
An imprint of Lerner Publishing Group, Inc.
241 First Avenue North
Minneapolis, MN 55401 USA

For reading levels and more information, look up this title at www.lernerbooks.com.

Main body text set in Memphis Pro 24/39
Typeface provided by Linotype.

Photo Acknowledgments
The images in this book are used with the permission of: © Serhii Prystupa/Adobe Stock, p. 3; © mspoli/Shutterstock Images, pp. 4–5, 16 (middle); © Cavan/Adobe Stock, pp. 6–7; © Maridav/Adobe Stock, pp. 8–9, 16 (right); © DreamHack/Shutterstock Images, pp. 10–11; © Victoria Kurylo/Shutterstock Images, pp. 12–13, 16 (left); © Michael Tatman/Shutterstock Images, pp. 14–15.

Front cover: © Magenta Dream/Adobe Stock

Library of Congress Cataloging-in-Publication Data

Names: Chu, Katherine, author.
Title: Recycled gardens / written by Katherine Chu.
Description: Minneapolis : Lerner Publications, [2025] | Series: In the garden (pull ahead readers – nonfiction) | Includes index. | Audience: Ages 4–7 | Audience: Grades K–1 | Summary: "Give back to the Earth by gardening with old objects! This engaging and carefully leveled text shows emergent readers how they can recycle in their garden. Pairs with the fiction title Growing Upward"— Provided by publisher.
Identifiers: LCCN 2024009495 (print) | LCCN 2024009496 (ebook) | ISBN 9798765647783 (lib. bdg.) | ISBN 9798765661994 (pbk.) | ISBN 9798765655559 (epub)
Subjects: LCSH: Gardening--Juvenile literature. | Recycling (Waste, etc.)—Juvenile literature.
Classification: LCC SB454.3.R43 C48 2025 (print) | LCC SB454.3.R43   (ebook) | DDC 635—dc23/eng/20240423

LC record available at https://lccn.loc.gov/2024009495
LC ebook record available at https://lccn.loc.gov/2024009496

Manufactured in the United States of America
1 – CG – 12/15/24

Table of Contents

Recycled Gardens 4

Did You See It? 16

Index 16

Recycled Gardens

I use old cans in my garden.

I use old boots in my garden.

I use old jars in my garden.

I use old bags in my garden.

I use old baskets in my garden.

I recycle in my garden!

Did You See It?

basket   can   jar

Index

bags, 11   cans, 5

baskets, 13   jars, 9

boots, 7   recycle, 15